Fresh Start

Dear Friends,

Welcome to the **"Fresh Start"** Bible study series! My name is Brian, and I am truly excited that you've decided to join me on this journey of discovering what it means to embrace each new day with hope, faith, and a renewed sense of purpose. This study was designed with a simple truth in mind: no matter what happened yesterday, God offers us a fresh start every day. His mercies are new each morning, and He gives us the grace to move forward with confidence, knowing He's walking with us every step of the way.

Throughout these eight sessions, we will explore how God invites us to release the past, live fully in the present, and trust Him with our future. We will dive into scripture, engage in meaningful discussions, and participate in activities that help us apply these truths to our daily lives. Whether you are coming to this study from a place of strength or struggle, I believe there is something here for you.

As we walk through themes like forgiveness, hope, faith, and renewal, my prayer is that you will experience God's presence in a deeper way. I hope that by the end of this study, you will have a renewed mindset, a strengthened faith, and the courage to step forward into the fresh start that God offers each of us.

Thank you for joining me on this journey. I encourage you to engage fully, ask questions, share your thoughts, and allow God to work in your life through this study. It's my privilege to walk alongside you as we discover what it means to live each day as a fresh start in Christ.

If you have found this study beneficial,
please explore our other studies available
on Amazon. Scan the QR code or go to:
www.amazon.com/author/adams.brian1

Blessings,

Brian

Small Group Guidelines

Review these guidelines at the start of each session.

1. **Confidentiality:** What is shared in the group stays in the group. Respect each other's privacy to foster a safe and trusting environment.

2. **Respect for All Voices:** Encourage everyone to participate and share their thoughts. Respect differing opinions and listen without interrupting.

3. **Punctuality:** Arrive on time and stay for the entire session. Value each other's time and commitment to the group.

4. **Preparation:** Come prepared having read the assigned scripture or materials. This shows respect for the group's time and enhances the discussion.

5. **Prayerful Support:** Begin and end each session with prayer. Offer to pray for one another, respecting individual prayer requests and needs.

6. **Stay on Topic:** Keep discussions focused on the designated scripture or topic. This ensures that conversations are productive and beneficial for everyone's spiritual growth.

7. **Encourage Growth:** Challenge each other to apply biblical teachings to daily life, but do so with kindness and encouragement.

8. **No Judgement:** Foster an atmosphere where questions and doubts can be expressed without fear of judgment. Remember, we are all on a journey of faith and learning.

9. **Conflict Resolution:** Address disagreements or conflicts within the group promptly and biblically, always aiming for reconciliation and unity.

10. **Celebrate Milestones:** Acknowledge the group's progress and individual growth. Celebrate milestones and encourage one another in your spiritual journeys.

By adhering to these guidelines, your Bible study group can create a nurturing and enriching environment that promotes spiritual growth and strong community bonds.

Table of Contents

Session 1: A New Beginning Every Morning

Opening Prayer.

Heavenly Father,

We come before You with grateful hearts, thankful for the gift of today and the new mercies You provide each morning. As we begin this journey of discovering fresh starts in You, we ask for Your presence to guide and inspire us. Help us to leave behind the burdens of the past and open our hearts to the possibilities that each new day holds. Lord, we invite Your Holy Spirit into this space—teach us, renew us, and transform our thinking so that we may live each day fully in Your grace. May Your Word speak to us clearly today and bring hope and encouragement to every heart.

In Jesus' name, we pray,

Amen.

Session Introduction:

Understanding the concept of daily renewal and God's new mercies each day.

Scripture Reading:

Lamentations 3:22-23 – God's mercies are new every morning.

Psalm 118:24 – Today is the day the Lord has made.

2 Corinthians 5:17 – In Christ, we are a new creation.

Reflection:

Each verse emphasizes that every day brings new opportunities, regardless of yesterday's struggles. How does this impact our attitude toward starting fresh?

Discussion Points:

What does a "new beginning" mean to you?

How can we let go of yesterday's mistakes to embrace today?

In what ways does God's mercy impact your daily life?

How do you experience the renewal of God's grace?

Why is it difficult to accept that today can be different from yesterday?

Activities:

Group discussion: Share a personal experience of starting fresh after a tough time.

Journaling: Reflect on an area where you need a new beginning.

Prayer circle: Pray for God to help you embrace today and release the past.

Session Recap:

A summary of key insights about embracing new beginnings daily.

Closing Prayer.

Loving Father,

Thank You for reminding us that Your mercies are new every morning and that we can always find a fresh start in You. We are so grateful for the opportunity to learn from Your Word today, and for the way You are working in each of our lives. As we go forth from this session, help us to embrace the truth that today is a new day, a gift from You, and an opportunity to live in Your love and grace. Empower us to release yesterday's burdens and face tomorrow with hope and faith in Your promises. We ask for strength, courage, and a renewed sense of purpose as we live out our faith day by day.

In Jesus' name,
Amen.

Homework:

Scripture Memory Verse: Lamentations 3:22-23.

Daily Reflection: How will you embrace God's new mercies tomorrow?

Notes Section:

Space for personal reflections, insights, and additional thoughts from the session.

Session 2: Letting Go of Yesterday

Opening Prayer.

Gracious Father,

We come before You today, thankful for the chance to gather and learn from Your Word. We know that sometimes we carry the weight of yesterday with us, and it holds us back from fully embracing the new things You have for us today. Lord, as we dive into Your scriptures, help us to understand the power of letting go of the past. Open our hearts to release the burdens and hurts that weigh us down and fill us with the peace that comes from trusting You with our future. We ask for Your grace and wisdom in this time, and we invite Your presence to be with us as we learn more about living freely in You.

In Jesus' name,
Amen.

Recap of Previous Session:

Last week, we explored how God's mercies are new every morning and how we can embrace each day as a new beginning. What stood out to you about the idea of starting fresh each day?

Homework Review:

Review the scripture memory verse (Lamentations 3:22-23) and discuss reflections on embracing God's mercies each day.

Session Introduction:

This session focuses on the challenge of letting go of past baggage and moving forward with faith. We will explore how Scripture encourages us to release the past so we can fully embrace the future that God has planned for us.

Scripture Reading:

Philippians 3:13-14

Forgetting what is behind and pressing on toward the goal.

Matthew 6:34

Do not worry about tomorrow, as today has enough trouble of its own.

Hebrews 12:1-2

Throw off everything that hinders and run with perseverance.

Reflection:

These scriptures show the importance of leaving behind burdens and focusing on what lies ahead. We can't live in the past and the future at the same time, and God calls us to move forward in faith.

Discussion Points:

Why is it difficult to let go of past mistakes or hurts?

How does holding on to the past impact our ability to move forward with God's purpose?

What are some practical steps you can take to let go of yesterday's baggage?

How can you trust God more with your future rather than worrying about what's behind you?

How does focusing on today help us experience more of God's presence and peace?

Activities:

Group Discussion:

Share personal experiences of holding on to the past and how you were able to move forward.

Prayer Exercise:

Write down one thing from your past you are struggling to let go of. Pray together for God's help in releasing it.

Scripture Reflection:

Meditate on Philippians 3:13-14 and share how it can inspire you to press forward without looking back.

Session Recap:

Summarize key points about letting go of yesterday and trusting God with the future. Highlight how releasing the past allows us to fully live in God's grace for today.

Closing Prayer.

Heavenly Father,

Thank You for the truth and freedom found in Your Word. We are grateful for the reminder today that we do not have to hold on to the past because You are always calling us forward into something new. Lord, give us the strength to release the things that no longer serve us—whether it's guilt, mistakes, or past hurts—and to trust that You have a plan for our future. As we leave this place, let us carry the peace that comes from letting go and stepping into the fresh start You offer each day. Help us to trust in Your goodness and to walk forward with renewed hope and faith.

In Jesus' name,

Amen.

Homework:

Scripture Memory Verse: Philippians 3:13-14.

Daily Reflection: What is one thing you will leave behind from yesterday to fully embrace God's new opportunities for today?

Notes Section:

Space for personal reflections, insights, and additional thoughts from the session.

Session 3: God's Grace for Today

Opening Prayer.

Heavenly Father,

We gather in Your presence today, thankful for Your never-ending grace. We know that each day brings its own challenges, but You provide all that we need to face them. As we focus on Your Word and learn about Your grace for today, we ask that You open our hearts and minds to fully receive this truth. Help us to depend on You daily, knowing that Your grace is always sufficient for us. Teach us to let go of anxiety about tomorrow and trust in Your provision for today. Let this time be filled with Your peace and wisdom.

In Jesus' name,
Amen.

Recap of Previous Session:

Last week, we discussed the importance of letting go of yesterday and pressing forward. What insights did you gain about releasing past burdens and embracing the future?

Homework Review:

Review the scripture memory verse (Philippians 3:13-14) and discuss reflections on letting go of past baggage and focusing on today.

Session Introduction:

This session emphasizes the sufficiency of God's grace for today. We will explore how God provides everything we need for each day and how we can learn to depend on His grace moment by moment.

Scripture Reading:

Matthew 6:11 – "Give us today our daily bread."

2 Corinthians 12:9 – "My grace is sufficient for you."

Psalm 68:19 – "Praise be to the Lord, to God our Savior, who daily bears our burdens."

Lamentations 3:22-23 – "His mercies are new every morning."

Reflection:

These scriptures highlight God's provision and grace for each day. We do not need to worry about tomorrow because God meets our needs today.

Discussion Points:

What does it mean to rely on God's grace daily?

How does focusing on today help alleviate worries about the future?

In what ways have you experienced God's grace carrying you through difficult times?

What are practical ways to remind yourself to seek God's grace each day?

How can we encourage others to trust in God's daily provision?

Activities:

Group Discussion:

Share a time when you had to fully rely on God's grace for a particular day. What did you learn from that experience?

Daily Grace Journal:

Start a daily journal where you write down moments where you see God's grace and provision in your life.

Prayer Circle:

Pray for each other, specifically asking God to help each participant rely on His grace more fully each day.

Session Recap:

Summarize key points about God's daily grace and how He provides exactly what we need for each day, not more and not less.

Closing Prayer.

Loving Father,

Thank You for reminding us of the abundance of Your grace. As we leave this session, we carry with us the assurance that You are with us in every moment, providing exactly what we need. Help us to lean into Your grace, not just when life feels difficult, but every day, knowing that Your strength is made perfect in our weakness. Lord, we ask that You give us the courage to let go of our worries about tomorrow and trust You for today. As we go through the week, may we remember that Your grace is more than enough.

In Jesus' name,
Amen.

Homework:

Scripture Memory Verse: 2 Corinthians 12:9.

Daily Reflection: In what area of your life do you need to rely more on God's grace?

Notes Section:

Space for personal reflections, insights, and additional thoughts from the session.

Session 4: Renewing Your Mind

Opening Prayer.

Heavenly Father,

We come before You with open hearts and minds, ready to receive Your truth. Today, as we focus on the renewal of our minds, we ask for Your wisdom and guidance. Help us to see the areas in our lives where we need transformation, and give us the courage to embrace the change that comes from aligning our thoughts with Your Word. Lord, let Your Holy Spirit renew our minds so we may live in a way that reflects Your love and purpose. Thank You for the opportunity to grow and be made new in You today.

In Jesus' name,

Amen.

Recap of Previous Session:

Last week, we focused on God's grace for each day and how He provides for us. What stood out to you about relying on God's grace daily?

Homework Review:

Review the scripture memory verse (2 Corinthians 12:9) and discuss reflections on areas in your life where you need to rely more on God's grace.

Session Introduction:

This session focuses on the importance of renewing our minds. In order to live a "fresh start" each day, we must transform our thinking to align with God's truth. The renewing of our mind is essential for spiritual growth and experiencing newness in Christ.

Scripture Reading:

Romans 12:2 – "Do not conform to the pattern of this world, but be transformed by the renewing of your mind."

Ephesians 4:22-24 – "Put off your old self... and be made new in the attitude of your minds."

Colossians 3:9-10 – "Do not lie to each other, since you have taken off your old self with its practices and have put on the new self, which is being renewed in knowledge."

Philippians 4:8 – "Whatever is true, noble, right... think about such things."

Reflection:

These scriptures emphasize that the transformation of our minds is key to living a life that reflects God's will. By focusing on God's truth, we can change our thought patterns and live with a renewed perspective each day.

Discussion Points:

What does it mean to "renew your mind"?

How does the world's way of thinking differ from God's truth?

What practical steps can we take to renew our minds daily?

In what areas of your life do you find it difficult to align your thoughts with God's truth?

How does renewing your mind affect your relationship with God and others?

What are some influences that hinder the renewal of your mind (media, social interactions, etc.)?

How can focusing on scripture help in the renewal process?

Activities:

Mind Renewal Exercise: Write down a negative or unbiblical thought you struggle with, and then find a Bible verse that speaks truth into that situation.

Group Discussion: Share personal strategies for mind renewal and how they've impacted your spiritual life.

Scripture Meditation: Choose one of the verses from today's session and spend 5 minutes meditating on it. Reflect on how you can apply it to your life.

Session Recap:

Review the significance of renewing your mind and how it can lead to a fresh start each day. Emphasize the importance of daily transformation by aligning our thoughts with God's truth.

Closing Prayer.

Gracious Father,

Thank You for teaching us today about the importance of renewing our minds. As we move forward from this session, help us to meditate on Your truth daily, allowing our thoughts to be transformed by Your Word. Let us reject the patterns of this world and instead embrace the mindset You desire for us. May Your Spirit guide our thoughts and actions so that we reflect Your love and grace in everything we do. We ask that You strengthen us to continue this journey of transformation, renewing our minds each day through Your truth.

In Jesus' name,
Amen.

Homework:

Scripture Memory Verse: Romans 12:2.

Daily Reflection: What is one negative thought pattern you will work on renewing this week with God's truth?

Notes Section:

Space for personal reflections, insights, and additional thoughts from the session.

Session 5: Forgiveness and New Beginnings

Opening Prayer.

Heavenly Father,

We come before You today with humble hearts, recognizing our need for Your forgiveness and grace. As we learn about the power of forgiveness and the fresh start it brings, we ask that You open our hearts to fully receive and extend forgiveness. Help us to let go of any bitterness or resentment that may be holding us back from the new beginnings You have for us. Fill us with Your love so we can forgive others as You have forgiven us. Guide our time together and speak to us through Your Word.

In Jesus' name,
Amen.

Recap of Previous Session:

Last week, we discussed the importance of renewing your mind and aligning your thoughts with God's truth. How has focusing on renewing your mind impacted your week?

Homework Review:

Review the scripture memory verse (Romans 12:2) and discuss how participants have applied mind renewal in their lives.

Session Introduction:

This session will focus on forgiveness—both receiving it from God and extending it to others—as a key part of starting fresh. Forgiveness is essential for leaving the past behind and embracing new beginnings. Without forgiveness, we remain bound by our past mistakes and hurts.

Scripture Reading:

Ephesians 4:31-32 – "Get rid of all bitterness... forgiving each other, just as in Christ God forgave you."

Matthew 18:21-22 – "How many times shall I forgive? Seventy times seven."

Colossians 3:13 – "Bear with each other and forgive one another if any of you has a grievance... forgive as the Lord forgave you."

1 John 1:9 – "If we confess our sins, He is faithful and just to forgive us our sins and purify us from all unrighteousness."

Reflection:

These scriptures show the importance of forgiveness in the Christian life. By receiving forgiveness from God and forgiving others, we allow ourselves to break free from the past and move forward into the future that God has for us.

Discussion Points:

Why is forgiveness essential for a fresh start?

What are some common obstacles to forgiving others?

How does holding on to bitterness and unforgiveness affect your spiritual life?

What steps can you take to forgive someone who has hurt you deeply?

How does receiving God's forgiveness help you extend forgiveness to others?

Why is it sometimes harder to forgive ourselves than others? How can we apply God's forgiveness to our own lives?

How can the act of forgiveness lead to emotional and spiritual freedom?

Activities:

Forgiveness Reflection: Write down someone you need to forgive or an area where you need to experience God's forgiveness. Pray for the strength to let go of any lingering bitterness.

Group Discussion: Share personal stories of times when forgiveness led to healing and renewal.

Forgiveness Prayer: Pray together for the strength to forgive and for the release of any unforgiveness that may be holding you back.

Session Recap:

Summarize the importance of forgiveness in the journey to a fresh start. Highlight how forgiving others and receiving God's forgiveness helps us break free from the past and embrace new beginnings.

Closing Prayer.

Loving Father,

Thank You for the powerful reminder of the freedom that comes with forgiveness. We are grateful for Your endless mercy and the new beginnings You offer us through Jesus. As we leave this session, help us to release any lingering bitterness or hurt and replace it with Your peace and love. Give us the strength to forgive others and ourselves, knowing that it is through forgiveness that we experience true freedom and healing. May Your grace fill our hearts as we continue this journey of fresh starts in You.

In Jesus' name,
Amen.

Homework:

Scripture Memory Verse: Ephesians 4:31-32.

Daily Reflection: Think of one area in your life where you need to extend forgiveness—either to yourself others, or accept God's forgiveness.

Notes Section:

Space for personal reflections, insights, and additional thoughts from the session.

Session 6: Hope for Tomorrow

Opening Prayer.

Heavenly Father,

We thank You for gathering us here today and for the hope You give us through Your promises. As we focus on the hope we have for tomorrow, help us to trust in Your plans, even when we can't see the path ahead. Lord, fill our hearts with peace and confidence, knowing that You are in control of our future. Teach us to rely on Your Word and to place our hope in You alone. Be present with us in this time, and guide our thoughts and discussions as we learn from Your truth.

In Jesus' name,

Amen.

Recap of Previous Session:

Last week, we explored the power of forgiveness in helping us move forward. How did practicing forgiveness impact your week?

Homework Review:

Review the scripture memory verse (Ephesians 4:31-32) and discuss how forgiveness was applied in daily life.

Session Introduction:

This session will focus on hope for tomorrow. Often, the baggage of yesterday can make it difficult to believe in the promises of a hopeful future. However, God's Word assures us that we can trust Him with our future, no matter what challenges we face.

Scripture Reading:

Jeremiah 29:11 – "For I know the plans I have for you... plans to prosper you and not to harm you, plans to give you hope and a future."

Romans 8:28 – "And we know that in all things God works for the good of those who love Him, who have been called according to His purpose."

Isaiah 40:31 – "But those who hope in the Lord will renew their strength."

Proverbs 3:5-6 – "Trust in the Lord with all your heart and lean not on your own understanding; in all your ways submit to Him, and He will make your paths straight."

Reflection:

These scriptures highlight God's sovereignty over our future and His plan for good, no matter the uncertainties we may face. Trusting God with our tomorrow gives us hope and a renewed sense of purpose.

Discussion Points:

How does knowing that God has a plan for your life impact your view of the future?

What are some areas of your life where you struggle to trust God with your future?

How can we hold on to hope even when our circumstances are challenging?

Why is it important to rely on God's promises instead of our own understanding of the future?

In what ways can we cultivate a hopeful mindset about tomorrow?

How has your faith been strengthened through seasons of waiting or uncertainty?

How does trusting in God's plans give you peace for the future?

Activities:

Hope Journal: Write down one area of your life where you need to trust God more in the future. Reflect on scriptures that offer hope and guidance.

Group Sharing: Discuss situations where you've seen God's plans for good unfold despite initial struggles or challenges.

Hope Prayer: Pray as a group for each other's futures, asking God to strengthen your hope in His plans and purposes.

Session Recap:

Review the significance of trusting God for tomorrow. Emphasize how hope in God's plans helps us face uncertainty with confidence and peace.

Closing Prayer.

Loving Father,

Thank You for the hope You give us, no matter what our circumstances look like. As we reflect on what we've learned today, we ask that You continue to strengthen our faith and trust in You for the future. Help us to rest in the assurance that You are working all things for our good and Your glory. Lord, guide our steps as we move forward, and remind us daily of the hope we have in You. May we leave this session with renewed confidence in Your promises and a heart filled with peace and hope.

In Jesus' name,
Amen.

Homework:

Scripture Memory Verse: Jeremiah 29:11.

Daily Reflection: What are you trusting God for in the future? How can you rest in His promises?

Notes Section:

Space for personal reflections, insights, and additional thoughts from the session.

Session 7: Living in the Present Moment

Opening Prayer.

Gracious Father,

We thank You for the gift of today. As we gather to learn about living in the present moment, help us to focus our hearts and minds on Your presence here with us. Teach us to let go of distractions, worries about the future, and regrets from the past so we can fully embrace the life You've given us today. Lord, help us to see the beauty of each moment and to live intentionally in Your grace. Open our eyes to the opportunities You have placed before us, and give us peace as we trust in Your timing.

In Jesus' name,

Amen.

Recap of Previous Session:

Last week, we talked about hope for tomorrow and trusting God with our future. How has focusing on hope changed your perspective on your circumstances?

Homework Review:

Review the scripture memory verse (Jeremiah 29:11) and discuss how you applied the promise of hope and trust in God's plan during the week.

Session Introduction:

This session will focus on the importance of living in the present moment. Often, we are either stuck in the past or consumed with worries about the future, but God calls us to live each day fully and intentionally. We'll explore how to embrace the present as part of our "fresh start" mindset.

Scripture Reading:

Matthew 6:33-34 – "But seek first His kingdom and His righteousness, and all these things will be given to you as well. Therefore, do not worry about tomorrow, for tomorrow will worry about itself."

Psalm 118:24 – "This is the day the Lord has made; let us rejoice and be glad in it."

James 4:14 – "Why, you do not even know what will happen tomorrow... you are a mist that appears for a little while and then vanishes."

Philippians 4:6 – "Do not be anxious about anything, but in every situation, by prayer and petition, with thanksgiving, present your requests to God."

Reflection:
These scriptures remind us of the fleeting nature of life and the importance of focusing on today rather than worrying about tomorrow. Living in the present allows us to trust in God's provision and celebrate the gift of each day.

Discussion Points:

Why is it difficult to stay present and not be consumed by the past or the future?

How does seeking God first help us live fully in the moment?

What are the dangers of worrying too much about tomorrow?

How can we practice gratitude for today, even when we are dealing with challenges?

What does it mean to "rejoice and be glad" in the day that the Lord has made?

How can we become more mindful of God's presence in our daily lives?

How does living in the present affect your relationship with others and with God?

Activities:

Present Moment Exercise: Write down three things you are grateful for today. Reflect on how living in the present brings joy and peace.

Group Sharing: Discuss how you've struggled or succeeded in living fully in the present during your week. Share practical tips that help you stay grounded in the moment.

Mindfulness Prayer: Spend a few minutes in silent prayer, focusing on God's presence right now. Ask Him to help you appreciate each day as a gift.

Session Recap

Summarize the importance of focusing on today and trusting God with tomorrow. Emphasize the value of living in the present moment and experiencing God's peace and joy today.

Closing Prayer

Heavenly Father,

Thank You for reminding us of the importance of living fully in the present. As we move forward, help us be mindful of each day You give us and find joy in the moments we often overlook. Teach us to trust You with tomorrow and to release the burdens of yesterday. May we seek You daily, knowing that You provide all that we need for today. Lord, let Your peace and presence guide us, and may we live each day with gratitude and purpose in Your will.

In Jesus' name,
Amen.

Homework:

Scripture Memory Verse: Matthew 6:33-34.

Daily Reflection: What can you do each day this week to be more mindful of God's presence and live fully in the present?

Notes Section:

Space for personal reflections, insights, and additional thoughts from the session.

Session 8: Stepping Forward in Faith

Opening Prayer.

Heavenly Father,

We come before You today with hearts open to Your guidance and grace. As we focus on stepping forward in faith, we ask that You give us the courage to trust You with our future. Help us to release any fear or doubt that holds us back and to walk boldly in the plans You have for us. Lord, remind us that You are with us in every step, and Your promises are true. May Your Spirit lead us during this time of learning and reflection, and may we leave this session with a renewed commitment to walk by faith.

In Jesus' name,
Amen.

Recap of Previous Session:

Last week, we discussed the importance of living in the present moment and trusting God with each day. How did focusing on the present change your perspective during the week?

Homework Review:

Review the scripture memory verse (Matthew 6:33-34) and discuss how participants practiced living in the present and trusting God for tomorrow.

Session Introduction:

This final session will focus on stepping forward in faith. While each day is a fresh start, it also requires faith to step into the unknown and trust God with our future. We'll explore how to have the courage to take action, trusting God even when the path ahead is uncertain.

Scripture Reading:

Joshua 1:9 – "Have I not commanded you? Be strong and courageous. Do not be afraid; do not be discouraged, for the Lord your God will be with you wherever you go."

Proverbs 3:5-6 – "Trust in the Lord with all your heart and lean not on your own understanding."

Hebrews 11:1 – "Now faith is confidence in what we hope for and assurance about what we do not see."

Psalm 37:23-24 – "The Lord makes firm the steps of the one who delights in Him; though he may stumble, he will not fall, for the Lord upholds him with His hand."

Reflection:

These scriptures highlight the importance of trusting God and having courage in uncertain times. Faith is about moving forward, even when we cannot see the whole picture, trusting that God is guiding our steps.

Discussion Points:

What does stepping forward in faith look like in your life?

How does fear of the unknown hold us back from experiencing the fullness of God's plans?

Why is it important to trust in God's guidance rather than our own understanding?

How can we develop a habit of relying on God in every step we take?

What areas of your life require more faith and trust in God's direction?

How does trusting in God's promises help us move forward with confidence and peace?

How can we encourage one another to step forward in faith when challenges arise?

Activities:

Faith Reflection: Write down an area in your life where you need to take a step of faith. Reflect on how you can trust God with that situation.

Group Sharing: Share a story of a time when stepping forward in faith led to God's provision and blessing.

Faith Prayer: Pray as a group for courage and strength to step forward in faith, trusting God to guide each person's steps.

Session Recap

Highlight the key points about stepping forward in faith and trusting God even when the future is unclear. Emphasize how faith is an active response to God's promises and guidance.

Closing Prayer.

Loving Father,

Thank You for the encouragement we've received today about stepping forward in faith. As we close this session, we ask that You continue to strengthen us and trust You more fully, especially when the path ahead is unclear. Lord, help us to take each step with confidence, knowing that You are guiding us and that Your plans for us are good. May we carry the lessons of faith, hope, and trust with us into our daily lives, and may we walk forward with boldness, assured of Your presence every step of the way.

In Jesus' name,
Amen.

Homework:

Scripture Memory Verse: Joshua 1:9.

Daily Reflection: What step of faith will you take this week, trusting God with your future?

Notes Section:

Space for personal reflections, insights, and additional thoughts from the session.